Kutusoff Nicolson Macfee

Imperial customs union, a practical scheme of fiscal union for the purposes of defence and preferential trade

From a colonist's standpoint

Kutusoff Nicolson Macfee

Imperial customs union, a practical scheme of fiscal union for the purposes of defence and preferential trade
From a colonist's standpoint

ISBN/EAN: 9783337151973

Printed in Europe, USA, Canada, Australia, Japan

Cover: Foto ©ninafisch / pixelio.de

More available books at **www.hansebooks.com**

IMPERIAL CUSTOMS UNION

A PRACTICAL SCHEME OF FISCAL UNION FOR THE
PURPOSES OF DEFENCE AND PREFERENTIAL
TRADE FROM A COLONIST'S STANDPOINT

BY

K. N. MACFEE, M.A., B.C.L.

LONDON
EFFINGHAM WILSON
ROYAL EXCHANGE, E.C.
1896

PREFACE.

THE fiscal union outlined in the following pages is submitted to the public as a simple and practicable plan of strengthening the ties which unite the several parts of the Empire, acceptable to protectionists, yet consistent with free-trade principles. During my long residence in Canada, the most protectionist of Colonies, I became convinced that moderate protection was beneficial to Colonies in the early years of their development, though free trade is unquestionably the most advantageous policy for Great Britain. In formulating this scheme I have avoided, on the one hand, the Scylla of extreme protection, and, on the other hand, the Charybdis of universal free trade.

The proposed union begins with free trade throughout the Empire in seven products—flour, wheat, mutton, cheese, tallow, hides and skins—which are important exports of nearly all the self-governing Colonies, and with a duty of either ten per cent. or fifteen per cent. upon the imports thereof from foreign countries. This duty produces about £5,000,000, which is used in a *pro rata* reduction of other taxation. It represents a protective bonus of about £2,000,000 annually in favour of British agriculture, and an equal amount as a stimulus to Colonial production. This is justified on free-trade principles as a measure of precaution against food famine in time of war, and as such is an increase of about six per cent. in our total expenditure for defence. It is offset, besides, by the proposal that the Colonies shall assume one-half the cost of the Imperial garrisons and forts at strategic points outside the British Isles, about £1,000,000 annually. In addition, the Colonies subject imports from the United Kingdom to the minimum tariff, which averages ten per cent. less than the maximum tariff imposed upon foreign imports. This confers a benefit upon British traders of about £800,000 annually, on the basis of the trade of 1894.

The governmental control is vested in a consultative inter-Colonial conference holding biennial meetings, and in an administrative council of Colonial agents in London.

K. N. MACFEE.

LONDON, 30*th* May, 1896.

TABLE OF CONTENTS.

CHAP.	PAGE
I. INTRODUCTORY	1

II. THE POLITICAL AND COMMERCIAL UNIONS OF THE PAST 5

 Sketch of the Achaian, Bœotian, and Ætolian Leagues, of the Hanseatic League, the Swiss Federation, the German Zollverein, and the Confederation of the United States of America.

III. IMPERIAL DEFENCE 16

 British and Colonial Systems—Table of Expenditures of each—Development of Colonial Feeling in favour of Assisting in Defence of the Empire—Necessity of United Action.

IV. GOVERNMENT AND CONTROL 28

 Natural Growth of Constitutional Systems—Inter-Colonial Conferences a Nucleus of the Consultative Branch of an Imperial Union—Colonial Agents General as Members of an Imperial Administrative Council—List of Inter-Colonial Conferences.

V. IMPERIAL TARIFFS 44

 Respective Merits of Free Trade and Protection Policies—Exports the Criterion of Prosperity—Table of Imports into United Kingdom of various Colonial Specialties—Table of Imports of Do. from Foreign Countries, and Amount of fifteen per cent. and ten per cent. Duties thereon—Do. from British Possessions with same Duties—British Agriculture—Objections Answered—Table of Imports of same Colonial Specialties into Colonies.

CHAP.		PAGE
VI. Colonial Tariffs	... ...	66

    Rapid Proportionate Growth of Colonial Foreign Commerce—Table of Imports of Manufactures into Colonies, with Percentages—Table of Colonial Duties—Proposed Maximum and Minimum Tariff into Colonies—Objections Answered—Treaties.

| VII. The Constitution of the Imperial Customs Union | ... ... | 82 |

CHAPTER I.

INTRODUCTORY.

THE political and commercial union of independent communities has been attempted with varying success at all periods of history, and numerous instances of such union may be cited as examples for our guidance. But in ancient and mediæval times the obstacles to be overcome were very different from those which beset a commercial union of the British Empire. In the former case the difficulties were chiefly material and objective, whereas those which we have now to encounter are largely sentimental and subjective. In earlier times the semi-civilised condition of the members of the organised union, the turbulent character of many of their citizens, the inefficient means of communication even between countries not widely separated from one another, and the consequent lack of frequent intercourse between the different members, all tended to render an organised union of independent communities most difficult. And when such a union was accomplished, the same influences tended to weaken the bonds by which they were at first joined. In modern times, however, the use of steam and electricity has eliminated distance and brought into intimate relationship communities between which, in earlier times, intercourse was almost impracticable. The development of international trade and the extended habit of foreign travel which characterises the citizen of modern civilised states have begotten a feeling of fellowship and an identity of interests between widely separated communities which make strongly for organised union. But with this elimination of material obstacles by the advancement of science, there have grown up sentimental and subjective principles of action which counterbalance to a large extent the centralising agencies of this greater freedom of intercourse. Among such principles of nationalistic action may be mentioned, on the one hand, the dogmatic belief entertained by the inhabitants of the British Isles of the universal efficacy and applicability of the principles of free trade, and, on the other hand, the strenuous maintenance by nearly all the continental nations of Europe, by the great majority of the British self-governing Colonies, and by the United States of America, of the benefits of a protective tariff as applied respectively to the peculiar circumstances of each of them. Therefore, in formulating a plan for the commercial union of the whole, or of a large portion of the British Empire, allowance must be made for obstacles arising from these diverse tenets of national belief, and means must be devised for overcoming such subjective difficulties. In studying the influences which operated in the creation of the political and commercial unions of the past, and in their continuance and extinction, the existence of war or peace, or the prospect of either, stands prominently forth as the most potent principle of action. The fear of external enemies and the pressure of war have, in nearly every case, brought about this political and commercial union of independent communities, and the bonds which united them have been strengthened or relaxed according as the influence of war was more or less perceptible. In times of peace such unions tended invariably to slacken; domestic difficulties between the members composing the union began to show themselves, resulting in some cases in open rebellion; and the centralising influences became reduced to a minimum. But when an attack from without threatened the members of the union jointly, or any of them individually, the bonds of union grew taut; the citizens of the respective communities made up their private quarrels and rivalries; and each member of the community became willing again to strengthen the central authority even to the diminution of local rights. The same results were observable whether the union was both political and commercial like the Everlasting League of Switzerland, or chiefly commercial like the Hanseatic League, as will be shown in detail later on. This inter-relation of a state of war, either actual or prospective, with conservancy of political or commercial union is the key to the formation of an Imperial Customs Union for the British Empire, and must hold the foremost place in any successful scheme for such a union.

CHAPTER II.

THE POLITICAL AND COMMERCIAL UNIONS OF THE PAST.

THE earliest instance of successful and widely diffused political and commercial union of which any details have come down to us is that of the Achaian League, which existed from B.C. 274 to B.C. 146. This union was formed of several Greek city communities which agreed to organise themselves into a league for mutual protection against external enemies, and in so doing to assign certain rights and certain control belonging to each member of the group as a sovereign community, to a central body which should exert authority over all the members of the league in those matters assigned to it. There was a central assembly of which the members were elected by the constituent cities; and this central assembly had control over everything relating to war and peace; but the separate cities were allowed great local autonomy, even to having themselves subject districts whose inhabitants had no direct share in the general federal citizenship. "It was an Achaian nation with a national assembly, a national government, and a national tribune to which every Achaian citizen owed allegiance."[1] But the cities were not municipalities, they were sovereign commonwealths. In all external matters the federal government reserved to itself full authority. No independent diplomatic action could be taken by the individual cities, though particular embassies were, on several occasions, allowed by licence of the federal government to the constituent cities. The central assembly was not a representative body, but a primary open meeting. Every free Achaian, thirty years of age, could vote and speak, no matter where he resided. The president of the assembly had large personal powers, and had a number of counsellors, analogous to a modern Cabinet, to advise him. These usually formulated the federal measures, and proposed them in the assembly. The main object of this union was, however, political rather than commercial, and we do not hear of any measures of commercial import being passed by the federal assembly. The constituent cities were requisitioned for troops and moneys as they were required, but we do not know of any special powers conferred upon the assembly to enforce its ordinances, nor of any penalties prescribed against cities which refused to comply with the demands

[1] Freeman's *Federal Government*, p. 253.

of the federal power. We read of two cities refusing to pay the federal contributions, but we have no information as to whether they were coerced into doing it. For this reason it was chiefly a feeling of self-interest which kept the union intact; and in time of peace, when the incentive to union was very slight, we find that the federal power greatly weakened, but in time of storm and stress the constituent cities drew more closely together, and obeyed with alacrity the behests of the federal authority. The Achaian League was weakened, " indeed it finally perished by nothing so much as by the attempt to retain members in the federation against their will ".[1] Many points of resemblance between this constitution and that of the British Empire may be indicated. Every British Colonist exerts an influence politically upon the Imperial Parliament, when, and only when, he resides in the United Kingdom. So the Achaian citizen had to be present at the capital in order to make good his vote. Certain British Colonies have also occasionally been allowed to nominate representatives who were practically ambassadors. The union of the British Empire is kept intact mainly by a feeling of self-interest and of patriotic loyalty, as was the case with the Achaian League.

[1] Freeman's *Federal Government*, p. 119.

In the Bœotian League, and the Ætolian League, the same principles were manifest, and they give us no further light upon the successful management of a union of independent communities.

These various leagues differed somewhat in their principles of union. The Achaian League gave each city an equal vote; the Bœotian League gave Thebes two votes, and each of the other cities one. The Lycian League gave votes, some one, some two, and some three, according to the size of the cities.

Prof. Freeman says,[1] "All federations except the German Empire (and that is a federation only in form) have been formed by a number of small states which agreed in the face of some greater power that threatened them to become one state for all purposes that touched their relations to other powers. This description suits all the main federations of the world, old and new."

. The lessons we learn, therefore, from the several Greek federations are, that they were originally constituted for the purpose of defence; that the bonds became tighter in times of trouble, and relaxed in times of peace; and that these various unions attained great power, carried on successful wars and maintained their federal independence through several generations, though the individual

---

[1] Freeman's *Greater Greece, Greater Britain*, p. 52.

members of each federation were bound simply and voluntarily by a bond which they considered themselves at liberty to sever whenever their own interests should so dictate.

The history of Rome shows us the acme of centralisation, with the minimum of commercial development, while the story of Carthage displays the same extreme centralisation with a wide range of commercial development. But in the former case, and probably in the latter case also,[1] "each community retained for the most part its own commercial laws and customs duties, which operated to some extent in impeding the free interchange of their diverse commodities". Customs duties were established for revenue, not protection, and duties were paid back in case of re-exportation or lack of sale. In neither case was there any scope for a political or a commercial union.

The most interesting experiment for the purpose of our subject was that of the Hanseatic League, which comprised from sixty to eighty cities, and which was both a political and a commercial union. These cities were divided into four leading divisions, each division being grouped around its chief city, —Lubeck, Cologne, Brunswick, and Dantzic. A congress met every three years and comprised

[1] Merivale's *History of Rome*, vol. viii., p. 356.

deputies from the various towns. It was a deliberative assembly. When their deliberations were completed, the decrees were formally communicated to the magistrates of the city at the head of each circle, by whom they were communicated to the minor cities. The deputies always insisted upon referring every important matter to the town council at home, as their own powers were insufficient. "It was only in time of danger that the league displayed any real consistency; when the immediate danger was withdrawn, the want of union soon made itself again manifest. The towns joined the league of their own accord, but never considered themselves bound to send deputies to the general assemblies." [1]

Notwithstanding the voluntary character of their association, for three centuries the Hanseatic League held together, and not infrequently sacrificed their individual advantages for the common good. Their primary purpose was to promote the commerce of the federated towns, and to defend the highways and waterways of commerce. The penalty for non-observance of their decrees was expulsion from the league, and as the advantages of commerce and of protection were important, especially in time of war,

[1] *Encyclopædia Britannica*, art. "Hanseatic League"; MacCulloch, art. *Foreign Quarterly*, 1831, p. 132.

this constituted a menace against non-compliance with the federal decrees. Commerce was free between the several cities of the league, and they obtained many very valuable privileges in foreign countries in regard to the establishment of manufactories and banks. "In the fourteenth century the Hanseatic League changes from a union of merchants abroad to a league of towns at home. The league thus formed could scarcely have held long together, or displayed any federal unity, but for the pressure of external dangers."[1]

The constituent cities were requisitioned for moneys to carry on the war, but the weakness of the federal assembly made it largely a question of bargaining between the general assembly and the constituent cities, when each levy or tax was imposed, as to the proportionate amount of each. The rivalry of the English and Dutch and the discovery of America eventually weakened the league, and gradually most of the towns broke away, the last assembly being held in 1669.

The German Zollverein is another instance of a successful Customs League. In this case the contracting states, with Prussia taking the lead, entered into a Zollverein which provided that perfect freedom of commerce should be established between the contracting states; that duties on

---

[1] *Encyclopædia Britannica*, art. "Hanseatic League".

importation, exportation, and transit should be identical; that these should be charged along the frontier of the dominion of the contracting parties; and that each should participate in the produce of such duties in proportion to population. There were a few exceptions, such as patents, copyrights, and monopolies. This was an ideal Customs Union, providing for free trade within the territories of the league, and a uniform tariff against all foreign countries. An assembly of representatives, one from each of the allied states, met annually to hear complaints and to adjust difficulties; they had to be unanimous in their decisions. This union eventually merged into the present German Empire, in which the same principles are now in force.

The story of Swiss development from the original union of the three forest communities into the Everlasting League "for the purpose of self-defence against all who should attack or trouble them," until the new constitution of 1848, is a striking manifestation of the principle that the federal bond is strained almost to the point of snapping in times of peace and prosperity, but is tightened and strengthened in periods of danger from external attack. A learned writer states: "The original contrasts between the social condition of the different members of the league became very marked when the period of conquest began and led to quarrels which a few years later ripened into civil war ".[1]

At first common action was limited to the meeting of two envoys from each member of the league, and one from each of the *Socii*, or dependent associates in the diet. The powers of this diet included foreign relations, war, and peace, and common arrangements as to police, pestilence, customs duties, coinage, etc., but they entailed frequent references to the representative Government, which gave their envoys very slight powers. The decision of the majority did not bind the minority save in the case of the affairs of the bailiwicks ruled in common. Thus everything depended upon common agreement and good-will, but quarrels arose as to a division of conquered lands. During the seventeenth and eighteenth centuries the country was distracted by religious wars, and very little progress was made in political or commercial development. But in 1798 a paper constitution was imposed upon the Swiss Confederation by the French Republic. This was re-modelled in 1802 by Buonaparte and was subsequently changed in 1815 by the Vienna Congress, which gave to each of the twenty-two cantons one vote in the diet wherein an absolute majority decided all questions except foreign affairs,

[1] *Encyclopædia Britannica*, art. "Switzerland".

and for this three-fourths majority was required. In 1848 the present constitution was adopted, modelled largely upon that of the United States of America. This union has free trade among all the members of the federation, and a uniform tariff as regards foreign countries.

The United States of America was also constituted by pressure of external danger and was threatened with disruption at the time of its highest prosperity by reason of internal conflicts as to powers of the federal government. It also has free trade within its borders, and a uniform tariff against foreign countries.

Our examination of the various federations and unions of ancient, mediæval, and modern times has therefore established the following generalisations:

1. That the fear of external attack has been the potent influence to create such unions.

2. That though in times of peace the bonds of union tended to become relaxed, yet in nearly every case the recurrence of external danger strengthened anew these bonds.

3. That the federal authority had generally very slight powers of compelling the obedience of the constituent communities.

4. That the feeling of mutual interest, and the desire to do what was just and right, sufficed generally to produce compliance with the requirements of the central authority.

5. That commercial affairs did not engross the attention of the federal assemblies, and that the ultimate effect of such union was free trade within the boundaries of the union, and a uniform tariff as against foreign countries.

CHAPTER III.

IMPERIAL DEFENCE.

THE freedom from fear of attack during a long period of fourscore years has begotten a sense of security on the part of all British subjects which it is difficult to counteract. And this sense of security permeates even more completely the minds of the Colonists than of the Mother Country, because during that time they have practically grown from infancy to manhood, and retain no impression of the danger which may have menaced them in childhood. But occasionally the political atmosphere becomes surcharged with electrical war excitement, and their special attention is devoted for a short time to the question of imperial defence. The separate character of the British Empire, the gigantic commerce which it carries on in all parts of the world, and the energy and aggressiveness of its citizens demand commensurate methods of defence. This defence necessitates military and naval forces and requires the greater preponderance of the latter. Each class of forces must be disposed throughout the empire according to the respective requirements of each part. The army comprises two distinct classes, *viz.*, that which is maintained continuously in service, and that which combines military duties with civil occupations. The latter is essentially an army of defence and cannot be moved outside of the Colony or country in which it is trained. It comprises the volunteers and militia of the United Kingdom, paid out of the revenues of the United Kingdom; the volunteers and militia of Canada, paid by the Government of Canada; and the militia and volunteers of the other Colonies, paid by their respective Governments. The former is our movable army, which numbers about 219,400 officers and men, and is used to guard the most important and most vulnerable portions of the empire. A large part is kept continuously in India, which pays the total cost of the portion kept there. Another large contingent is kept in the United Kingdom as a reserve force in case of attack, while a few battalions are centred at points of strategic importance throughout the world to guard the lines of communication between the Mother Country and the Colonies.

As regards the navy, it is practically all maintained by the United Kingdom. The people of Australia have several gunboats which are manned by British officers and men, but are paid for by a fixed annual subvention from the Australasian

Colonies to the British Government. The proportion of expense, therefore, paid by the Colonies for the maintenance of the navy is infinitesimal, the Mother Country having to pay almost the whole. The proportion is estimated at about 19s. 6d. to 6d., that is as 39 to 1. The Colonies have become so accustomed to the idea that the navy is the British navy, that its maintenance at its present state of efficiency is essential for the protection of the commerce of Great Britain, and that the existence of the Colonies as Colonies does not increase the naval expenditure of the Mother Country by even one ship, that it becomes a serious problem to induce them to pay any larger share.

It cannot be doubted, if Great Britain were engaged in a war which threatened her Imperial position, that the Colonies would sacrifice their last man, and expend their last coin in coming to her rescue. This has been stated explicitly by Sir Julius Vogel and other prominent Colonial statesmen. The loyalty of the Canadians and their devotion to the empire are strikingly set forth in these noble words of the *Toronto Globe* in its issue of 21st December, 1895. Speaking of the bellicose message of President Cleveland respecting the Venezuela boundary, it says: " Grave as is the situation thus created for Canada, it is one which she accepts absolutely without murmuring. She will not complain that she will be involved in the consequences of a dispute with which she has no concern, because it is of her own free choice that she remains a member of a world-wide empire with world-wide responsibilities. In such a situation there is but one feeling, and that is a desire to co-operate heartily with Great Britain in her efforts to bring the controversy to a peaceful and honourable issue." The same sentiments were expressed by other Canadian papers. But in times of peace each Colony vies with the other in her endeavours to minimise her contributions to the general defence, and allows her sense of security to overshadow the duty of making preparation against attack. Besides, they have come to rely upon the Mother Country for naval protection. When the Colonies were granted self-government, the Imperial Parliament omitted to give it subject to the payment of a *pro rata* share of the general defence of the empire. This omission was mentioned by the late Lord Beaconsfield as a matter of special regret. The Colonies are therefore like a son who has been set up in business for himself and who has been granted, say, the free use of his business premises. After a series of years he considers he has a prescriptive right to the continuation of the free occupancy of such premises, and the attempt to make him pay for them, or to eject him from them, would be resented as unjust treatment. In the same way the Colonies have come to regard the protection afforded by the Imperial fleet as their right without payment. In order to induce them to contribute their share of expenses it is necessary to enter into a new arrangement by which, for a consideration, the Colonies will undertake, in addition to other concessions, to pay a share of the burdens of Imperial defence. This consideration will be set forth in another chapter, and must partake of the nature of a preferential tariff upon Colonial produce coming into the United Kingdom. Other mutual advantages will also be set forth as inducements for the contracting parties to enter into such an agreement; at present, however, we are dealing simply with Imperial defence. The apprehension of a great war or of attack from external enemies may be necessary to induce the Colonies to enter into a new arrangement of this character. Still, a great deal may be done to create a feeling in favour of this proposal by pressing the question firmly and continuously upon the attention of the Colonies.

The amounts expended during the years 1892-93-94 (the last years in which full returns are at hand for all the British possessions) by the respective portions of the British Empire, with their populations and expenses per head, were as shown in the Table (page 21).

IMPERIAL DEFENCE.

Population.	Country.	Defence Expenditure, 1892-93.		Defence Expenditure per Head of Population.	Proportion of Defence Expenditure to Revenue.	Proportion of Defence Expenditure to combined Imports and Exports.	Total Defence Expenditure, 1893-94.
39,000,000	United Kingdom	For Militia and Volunteers, about Naval bases outside the United Kingdom, about Army (remaining expenses)	£2,000,000 2,000,000 13,587,772	1/- 1/- 7/-			
		Total Army Navy	£17,587,772 14,325,949	9/-			
		Total Army and Navy	£31,913,721	16/4	1 to 2·86	1 to 20·6	£17,802,800 14,240,100
5,000,000	Canada		£293,600	1/2½	1 to 27	1 to 173	32,042,900 237,000
4,250,000	Australasia		907,311	4/3	1 to 38·1	1 to 137	737,129
2,100,000	Cape Colony and Natal	Cape Colony Natal	£344,270 76,810				
		Total Colonies	£1,621,991	4/- 3/-	1 to 18	1 to 67·5	446,831 1,420,960

From the Blue Books of the respective countries; and, as to Australasia, from Victorian Year Book—1893, p. 380; 1894, p. 807.

Canada expended for defence from 1868 to 1893 inclusive £7,000,000. Australasia to 1893 had incurred a debt for defence of £2,612,744, besides large expenditures out of annual revenue. These figures show that the United Kingdom pays a very much higher proportion than the Colonies, whether it is estimated as regards population or revenue, or combined exports and imports. In making a new arrangement it would no doubt be possible to induce the Colonies to increase their proportion, just as a first step was made in 1887 when the Australasian Colonies agreed to contribute £126,300 annually, and the interest at five per cent., not exceeding £35,000 annually upon the capital outlay, for an Australian squadron to be built and manned by the British Admiralty. Such an increased contribution would probably be most easily obtained by asking the Colonies to undertake jointly with the United Kingdom the expense of the maintenance of the naval bases outside the United Kingdom, which amounts to about £2,000,000 per annum. These naval bases, maintained as Imperial naval stations, are: Simon's Bay, Trincomalee, Bermuda, Esquimault, Halifax, Malta, Gibraltar, St. Lucia, Hong Kong and Ascension. These are all points of strategic importance, and are quite as necessary for the protection of the sea-borne commerce of the Colonies as of that of the United Kingdom. To these might be added: Cyprus, Natal, Mauritius, Sierra Leone, St. Helena, Ceylon, Straits Settlements, Barbados, and Jamaica, all of which still possess Imperial garrisons. The total number of troops stationed in the Colonies is 32,000 men, towards the cost of which the Colonies contribute now about £250,000. If the expense of these naval bases and Imperial garrisons outside of Great Britain is fixed at £2,000,000 a year,[1] it should be possible to get the Colonies to pay one-half, which is the proportion they are now contributing to the erection of fortifications at Esquimault, Cape Town, Freetown, St. Helena, Singapore and Hong Kong, towards which the Imperial Government also now contributes about one-half the estimated cost.[2] This contribution would raise the annual expenditure of the self-governing Colonies upon defence from its present amount of £1,500,000 to £2,500,000.

The Colonies have gradually been worked up to the point of contributing more and more to their own defence and that of the Empire. In 1875 Lord Carnarvon asked two of the Australasian Colonies to contribute £4000 each towards the government of the Fiji Islands, but they declined.

[1] The amount estimated by Sir Charles Dilke and Spencer Wilkinson in their work on *Imperial Defence*, p. 181.

[2] The Colonial List for 1895, p. 19.

Since that time the several Australasian Governments have undertaken the payment of the maintenance of an Australian squadron, and have joined with the British Government in fortifying strategic points both in and out of their respective countries, which were deemed necessary for joint protection—for example, Albany in West Australia and Thursday Island off the coast of Queensland. Canada, too, has undertaken the suppression of a rebellion within her borders for which a few years ago she would have expected the assistance of Imperial troops. She has also subsidised the Canadian Pacific Railway, which is invaluable as an Imperial military route. Both the Australian Colonies and Canada voluntarily offered assistance to the Imperial Government at the time of the Egyptian campaign, and recently for the Ashanti and Soudan expeditions. It is therefore only a question of appealing to the Colonies in a proper manner, stimulated perhaps by an apprehension of attack, in order to induce them to contribute more largely than they do at present to the defence of the Empire. The reply made by the Colonies now to charges that they do nothing towards the defence of the Empire is a general denial, and not a plea (which would have been alleged a few years ago) that they are not under any obligation to do so. They now allege that they do contribute a fair share towards Imperial defence.

The serious results which would follow a defeat of the Imperial navy—results quite as important for the Colonies as for the Mother Country—must be manifest to all. The sea-borne commerce of the Colonies with foreign countries is increasing more rapidly than that with the United Kingdom, and the injustice of relying upon the British fleet to protect this foreign-Colonial commerce without any contributions from them, emphasises this demand for a larger contribution than that at present made. " Besides, the sea-borne commerce of the Colonies with Great Britain is increasing year by year, and the importance of these lines of communication being maintained at all times for that commerce is becoming. more fully realised. A total external trade of about £53,000,000 in 1800 has grown to £973,000,000 in 1893. In the same period the Colonial population needing communication with the United Kingdom has grown from about 2,750,000 to 21,000,000. The movement of this vast volume of trade is the life-breath of the Empire. Unless communication between the scattered members of the nation can be maintained, the Empire must be broken into fragments."
"It is true that the provision of an Australian squadron marks a distinct advance (upon the idea that defence can be localised), but it is not yet realised that the highest interests of Australasia might demand the employment of this squadron

thousands of miles from her shores. Strain every nerve to hold the vital communications of the Empire, prepare the army for offensive operations across the sea, make ready to defend at short notice against naval raids such ports as will be needed in war. These, in order of importance, are the measures by which alone the national safety can be secured."[1]

It is necessary therefore to render these strategic points more impregnable, and to increase their potential usefulness in time of war. Every year naval experts are clamouring for a larger expenditure of money upon these naval bases, and the contribution of the Colonies may at first take the form of increasing the effective strength of these strategic points in case of a war with a great naval power. And in like manner as the representations of the advantages of a Pacific cable have induced most of the Colonies to agree to contribute towards its construction, so there is little question but that they would consent to bear a larger share of these expenditures, especially if such increased expenditure were combined with mutual fiscal advantages. Such new departure might not be wholly effected until some war scare had arisen, but if the question were

[1] Sir George Clarke, in *Blackwood's Magazine*, June, 1895.

seriously and fully discussed during a time of peace, any excitement as to an outbreak of war would, without doubt, induce the immediate adoption of measures which had only been partially entertained in time of peace.

CHAPTER IV.

GOVERNMENT AND CONTROL.

THE successful governments are those which have grown up naturally, which have been evolved by the respective circumstances of time and place of each community. No practicable working constitution springs full grown like Minerva from the head of Jupiter. The attempts which have been made to establish a paper constitution have rarely, if ever, been fully successful. The great example of a ready-made constitution is that of the United States of America. But two of its chief features —those which include the essence of the working of the constitution—were not planned by those who created it. When the American constitution was formed the election of president was withdrawn from the direct control of the people, and was committed to a council of wise men, to be specially elected by the people. These were then quietly and with due deliberation to select the best man in the confederation to be its ruler. This feature of the American constitution was a subject of special pride upon the part of its founders, but it is well known that no such object has been attained. These men who were to have considered impartially the qualities of the best persons in the Republic, and to have chosen for leadership him who was wisest and best, are now simply formal mandatories to register their votes for the candidate who has received the largest number of votes by states at an election voted upon by universal suffrage.

In the practical working of the American constitution, the seat of power lies in the meetings of the primaries which are nowhere mentioned in the constitution nor in the discussions respecting the constitution. The primaries are simply informal meetings of the voters in small sub-divisions to choose delegates to the caucuses, or conventions, which elect the candidates for various offices. These meetings constitute the commencement of an election campaign, and upon the selection of the delegates by these primaries depends in the last resort the choice of the candidates who will represent either party in the great party contests. These meetings, or primaries, have been evolved by the circumstances of time and place as essential to the proper working of the constitution, just as under the British constitution the system of government by Cabinets responsible to Parliament has grown up without being prescribed by any written constitution. Similar instances almost *ad infinitum* from other constitutions may be adduced to confirm this generalisation. Therefore, in arranging for the government of an Imperial Customs Union, a successful plan is most likely to be found, if it is simply a development of rudimentary practices which have already begun to exhibit themselves. In seeking such practices, two important factors present themselves at once to our view. The first is the position which has gradually been acquired by the High Commissioner for one leading colony, Canada, and the Agents General for several of the other Colonies. The other factor is the Inter-Colonial Conference which began in 1857, and has been held more or less formally, and more or less regularly ever since. The Colonial representatives resident in London have now practically the character of ambassadors. When any question affecting the Colony represented by them arises, they seek an interview with the head of the Imperial department having charge of the matter in question, in precisely the same way that a foreign ambassador presents similar cases to the Foreign Minister. In fact, the Colonial representatives have been given even a higher position. The High Commissioner for Canada has been allowed to negotiate treaties—especially with France and Spain—as representative of the Imperial Government and assisted by the British ambassadors accredited to the respective courts, treaties which affect Canada alone and in which the remainder of the British Empire is not included. And the action of the Colonial representatives has heretofore been independent of one another, just as the ambassadors of foreign countries act alone. A tendency to combination is, however, now discernible among them. The project of constituting the Colonial representatives in London a committee of Colonial advice has been frequently advocated by eminent British statesmen, beginning with Earl Grey, and including the Marquis of Lorne, Lord Playfair, Sir Lintorn Simmons, Admiral Colomb, Sir Julius Vogel, Sir H. Drummond Wolff, Mr. Wm. Forster, Sir Henry Parkes, Sir Bartle Frere, Lord Beaconsfield, and the Rt. Hon. Mr. Chamberlain. The latter seems inclined to put this conception into practice.

In order to give greater force to the combined representations of the Colonial representatives, it would be necessary to give them an organisation as a council of advice to the Colonial Secretary similar to the committee on plantations which formerly performed an analogous service, a precedent pointed out by the Marquis of Lorne. This organisation should include the holding of meetings at stated periods, in which all matters affecting the Colonies might be discussed. The representatives should also have increased powers, especially the decision of technical changes in the minimum and maximum tariff which might be adopted for the whole Empire, as will be explained in another chapter. These powers would be similar to those exercised by the diet of the German Zollverein, which decided matters of detail rather than questions of principle. Further importance might be given to this council of Colonial representatives, by having one of their number chosen a member of the Cabinet Council of Defence organised in the Imperial Cabinet. The presence of a Colonial representative upon this Council of Defence would give the Colonies that representation which modern ideas have associated with taxation or imposed contributions. In a few years, a council of Colonial representatives would gain so decided an influence, and become so essential, that British statesmen would wonder they had ever been able to do without them. The effect upon the Colonies would be equally pronounced and equally salutary.

Objections to such a council of Colonial advice have been raised by Mr. John Morley, Lord Blatchford, Prof. Goldwin Smith and others. Mr. Morley's objections are: "That the Imperial politics of any one Colony must either be regulated by a vote of the majority of members of the Colonial Council (however unpalatable the decision arrived at may be to the Colony affected), or else the Crown will be enabled to exercise its own discretion, and so arrogate to itself the right to direct Colonial policy; that the council may be at variance with the Government and majority in the Colony, and that difficulties are much better solved as they arise by a conference with each Colonial agent, which allows the Government of the Colony to take part in the negotiations and settle on its own terms; and that Imperial questions which interest one Colony do not interest the others. For instance, South Africa is not interested in the Newfoundland fisheries, and Canada is not interested in the New Zealand black labour question."[1]

Lord Blatchford states that "there is no reason to suppose that the Colonies prefer to have Colonial questions of Imperial import settled by a representative council of advice rather than by their own agents".[2]

Prof. Goldwin Smith says that "Colonial representatives would soon get out of touch with the Colonies".[3]

To this it may be replied that the habit of acting in common gradually creates an interest in

[1] "The Expansion of England," by John Morley, *Macmillan's Magazine*, February, 1894.
[2] "The Integrity of the British Empire," by Lord Blatchford, *Nineteenth Century*, October, 1877.
[3] "The Expansion of England," by Prof. Goldwin Smith, *Contemporary Review*, April, 1884.

all that concerns the welfare of each other. For instance, before the confederation of the Canadian Dominion the people of British Columbia took no interest in the affairs of the people of Nova Scotia and had practically no communication with them. Now the questions which affect any one province react upon the public opinion of another. At the present time the question of sectarian schools in Manitoba is agitating the whole Dominion from British Columbia to Prince Edward Island, and upon it the decision as to which party shall govern the Dominion during the next five years will be made. In like manner an Imperial Customs Union managed by a council of the Empire including Colonial agents would gradually beget in each member the same keen interest in what concerns the remotest part of the Empire as in that which concerns its nearest Colonial neighbours.

The questions to be decided by the council of the Empire would largely be questions of Imperial policy which are at present decided by the Imperial Parliament and the Imperial Government; these Imperial decisions are now imposed upon the Colonies without giving them any voice in the matter. For instance, the question of copyright is one which is only quasi-Imperial and has been accorded by Imperial statute to the exclusive jurisdiction of the Canadian Parliament; yet when Canada passes a copyright act the Imperial Government refuses to allow it to become law. If this question were brought up before the council of Colonial advice and decided against Canada in the same way that it is at present, it would cause no greater feeling of irritation than under the present *régime*. It is difficult to mention any other subject which is more likely to cause irritation, or upon which the Colonial representatives could more justly protest, than that of copyright.

On the other hand, the increased strength which the unanimous adoption of any question of Imperial policy by such a council would give to the Imperial executive, immeasurably outweighs the petty disadvantage which might arise from the dissatisfaction of any individual Colonial representative. And the experience of the readiness with which Colonial Parliaments have endorsed the action of their representatives without such a council of advice indicates that when the decisions are announced with the weight of a Colonial council there will be even less hesitation. In the recent Franco-Canadian treaty a very strong agitation arose in Canada to prevent its ratification after it had been negotiated by the High Commissioner, but the influence of the Canadian representative and the representations of the honour of their country being pledged were sufficient to have it ratified. A similar risk of the non-ratification of the acts of representatives not sufficiently authorised is incurred in the working of nearly all other constitutions and has not affected their effectiveness. Instances were quoted above in chapter ii. in discussing the unions of previous times. The objections of Prof. Goldwin Smith and Lord Blatchford are contradicted by our experience of the Colonial agents who keep intimately in touch with their respective Colonies and by their advocacy of this change.

The other factor which we notice as an embryo method of control is the Colonial conferences. These began in 1857, when a meeting of the General Association for the Australian Colonies was held in London Tavern, Bishopsgate Street, on 15th July, Mr. W. G. Wentworth in the chair. Since that date these conferences have been growing in frequency and in formal recognition. The following is a list of some of the more important inter-Colonial conferences :—

1857. Meeting of the General Association for the Australian Colonies, London Tavern, Bishopsgate Street, E.C. Discussion as to representation of Colonies in the Imperial Parliament.

1863. Conference held at Melbourne at which a schedule of uniform duties was drawn up. Four Australasian Colonies were represented.

GOVERNMENT AND CONTROL. 37

1864. Conference of representatives of the Colonies of British North America for the adoption of a Canadian confederation act held at Quebec, Canada.
1866. Conference held at London, England, which resulted in the formation of the Dominion of Canada.
1867. Conference held at Melbourne at which six Colonies were represented. Resolutions were passed respecting mail subsidies and an agreement on the part of the Australasian Colonies to pay a moiety not exceeding £200,000 per annum.
1870. Royal Committee of Victoria on Federal Union of Australasia held at Melbourne.
1871. Conference at Westminster Palace Hotel on Imperial federation and other Imperial questions.
1871. Conference held at Melbourne.
1873. Conference held at Sydney. Resolutions were passed by a majority of one in favour of a uniform tariff on the basis of free trade. Arrangement of joint mail and steamship service. Attended by delegates from Australasian Colonies.
1876. Conference at Sydney for the promotion of cable communication to Australasia, which was successful.

1877. Conference held at Sydney to consider the duplication of the submarine cable.
1878. Conference held at Melbourne respecting submarine cable.
1880. Second Conference called "Inter-Colonial Conference" held at Melbourne.
1881. Conference held at Sydney to continue deliberations of the previous Melbourne conference.
1881. Conference of Inter-Colonial and British Chambers of Commerce, held at Westminster Palace Hotel, 19th to 21st July.
1883. Conference of Australasian premiers and their colleagues met at Sydney.
1886. A Federal Council of Australasia held at Hobart to discuss the question of Australasian federation.
1886. Conference held at the Colonial and Indian Exhibition, London.
1887. Official Inter-Colonial Conference, London, convened by the Hon. Edward Stanhope, which resulted in the agreement of Australasian Colonies to maintain an Imperial Australasian naval squadron.
1888. Conference of delegates from the Orange Free State, the Cape of Good Hope, and Natal, on Customs Union and railway extension.

GOVERNMENT AND CONTROL. 39

1889. Australasian Commercial Congress held at Melbourne.
1890. Australasian Federation Conference held at Melbourne.
1891. National Australasian Conference held at Sydney.
1891-2-3-4-5. Australasian Postal and Telegraph Conferences held at the respective Australasian capitals in turn.
1894. Official Inter-Colonial Conference held at Ottawa, which resulted in joint subsidies to cable construction and fast mail service through all-British territory.

These, however, were not all truly Imperial meetings, though nearly all tended to promote joint action between several Colonies in the subjects which brought them together. In 1887 an official Colonial conference was called together in London, by the Hon. Edward Stanhope, as a true Imperial conference which discussed a great many Imperial questions, and which resulted in an agreement between the Imperial Government and the Australasian Colonies, whereby the latter agreed to contribute to the naval defence of their coasts, and to pay an annual subvention of £126,000 for the maintenance of an Australian squadron as a division of the British navy, besides interest at five per cent. upon the cost of the vessels not exceeding £35,000 annually. Other

Imperial questions were also discussed and a mutual agreement arranged. In 1894 the second official conference was held at Ottawa, at which Lord Jersey attended as the nominee of the Imperial Government, and where several important resolutions were passed. This conference has resulted in the agreement of the Imperial Government and nearly all of the self-governing Colonies to join in the construction of an all-British Pacific cable, and in an agreement to subsidise a steamship and railway route from Great Britain to Australia, through Canada, as wholly British territory.

These conferences are therefore the nucleus of the legislative body, or diet, of an Imperial Customs Union. They have resulted in the one case in a joint undertaking for an increase of the Imperial fleet, and in the other case for a joint expenditure upon an Imperial cable and an Imperial fast mail service. It is quite practicable for future conferences to undertake and carry to a successful completion the more difficult task of regulating Imperial defence and arranging an Imperial tariff. It is necessary, however, to give these conferences greater powers and greater regularity. An Imperial statute should be passed convening a conference of the Empire every year, or every alternate year, and prescribing the method of election of delegates to it. This conference should meet in the United Kingdom and the several Colonies in turn, because the holding of such a conference arouses a great interest in inter-Colonial questions in the country where it is held. The most important result of the conference held at Ottawa last year was the enthusiasm created among the people of Canada upon inter-Colonial questions and the attention which Canadians were thereby induced to give to the affairs of the other British Colonies. Such biennial meetings would greatly stimulate the development of a universal Imperial sentiment, such as the Canadian sentiment which has been created throughout the whole of British North America by the Canadian Confederation.

But some real power must be given to these conferences or they will sink into impotence, as was the case with the Federal Council of Australia. Among its functions might be prescribed the selection of a Colonist—by preference a resident Colonial agent—to represent the Colonies in the Council of Defence of the Empire. The conference might also be given limited powers respecting the tariff and the decision of broad lines of policy respecting the defence of the Empire. It is true that the Colonial Governments would desire to retain the final decision upon grave questions of policy in their own hands, but the delegates to the conference would be the mandatories of the respective Colonial and British Governments, and the votes which they gave upon questions submitted to the conference would be those dictated by their respective Governments. Some real power might therefore be assigned to them. The function of the conference would, however, be chiefly consultative and not executive, but its recommendations would carry weight with the various Colonial Governments, as has been proved by the success of those already held. It might be that in cases in which the Colonies were not unanimous the dissenting Colonies would not carry out the recommendations of the majority. But we have seen in the history of the great federations and unions of the past that the decisions of the majority were almost universally carried out. And it would be very difficult for a single Colony to hold out against the collective British Imperial decisions. The first confederation of the United States of America, it is true, was a failure, partly because of the lack of power to enforce the decrees of the federal executive, but special circumstances contributed to its impotency, owing to the great diversity of interests of the individual states, and it forms no criterion of the success of this union.

The tendency of such a conference would be gradually to assume to itself greater and greater power, just as the House of Commons gradually drew to itself the most important powers of the

British constitution. The relation between the Colonial council and the Colonial conference would gradually become that between an administrative and an executive body, and the conference would rely upon the Colonial council to take the initiative of carrying out the resolutions passed by the Colonial conference. The conference and council might each eventually group itself into opposing parties, one or other having alternately the predominance. The efficiency of these two bodies would be increased if the Colonial agents were given seats in the House of Commons as representing the Colonies, without voting powers, just as the members of the French Cabinet, having seats in the Senate, are allowed to address the House of Deputies. The hegemony of the Mother Country, both in the conference and in the Colonial council, would strengthen the influence of both bodies, and give that weight to their decisions which would command acquiescence. No advantage would be given one Colony at the expense of another. The dominant influence of the United Kingdom would make for unanimity, and measures which were not likely to be generally acceptable would not be pressed, just as they are not now insisted upon with the Colonies. The prestige given by the support of the Colonies would increase greatly the influence of the Empire, and the habit of working together would maintain its integrity and ensure its permanence.

CHAPTER V.

IMPERIAL TARIFFS.

A FREE trade policy has been in force in the United Kingdom for fifty years, and during that time this country has increased wonderfully its foreign and domestic trade. Though English political economists have pressed the adoption of this system upon foreign nations with great force and ability, and though the statesmen and economists of other countries are not inferior to those of Great Britain in intelligence and practical business sense, yet not one convert has been made, but all foreign countries and nearly all the Colonies adhere to a protective fiscal policy. The prosperity of many of those protective countries justifies that policy in the same way that free trade may be upheld by the record of the United Kingdom. The marvellous development of the United States of America, of Victoria, and of Canada, and the progress which Germany is making in competing with Great Britain in neutral markets in the sale of her manufactured products, despite her conscription, show that prosperity is

IMPERIAL TARIFFS.

quite as constant a handmaid of a protective as of a free trade policy. In neither case does this result prove anything definite as to their respective advantages.

It is a fair inference, therefore, that while the free trade policy is suitable to the maintenance of British commerce, yet it does not possess the same adaptability to other countries, or at least that it does not impress other nations with such convincing force as would be expected were its efficacy a self-evident proposition. Its main principles for the purposes of this study may be shortly stated as follows :—

1. Customs duties, if any, to be so imposed that the whole benefit of the imposed taxation shall accrue to the national treasury.

2. That such duties shall be imposed upon as few articles as possible.

3. That they shall be paid as directly as possible by those upon whom the burden ultimately falls.

On the other hand :—

1. A protective policy may increase the burdens of the community without benefiting the common treasury to the extent which the protective duties enhance the prices of dutiable articles not imported.

2. The tendency of a protective tariff is to increase the number of articles upon which a duty is levied, because untaxed substitutes gradually

come into use, and the duties to be effective must be extended to them.

3. The tax is usually paid by a middleman several degrees removed from the consumer.

The advantages claimed for a protective tariff are :—

1. That it stimulates the introduction of new industries which—

    (a) Render the nation less dependent upon foreigners in time of war.

    (b) Utilise labour and capital which would otherwise be transplanted to a foreign country.

    (c) Give greater diversity of product, and of employment, thereby preventing ruin should disaster befall one chief staple.

    (d) Develop labour of the highest character in the place of simple unskilled labour.

2. In all branches of commerce, custom gradually establishes a fixed rate of profit below which traders refuse to deal, but it sometimes happens that this customary profit is reduced in order to meet special forms of competition. For instance, it is now claimed that the Indian competition has forced Lancashire cotton manufacturers to carry on their business at a rate of profit which a few years ago they would have considered greatly insufficient. Protectionists claim that the establishment of a protective tariff has a

similar effect upon outside traders, whose rate of profits is lowered in order to meet the competition of the protected manufacturer. Thus the people of the protected country do not pay for imported goods an excess price equal to the full duty, but that price is reduced to some extent by the increased competition. In other words, the producer pays part of the duty.

3. That the competition among the protected manufacturers eventually reduces prices to the free trade level, the chief benefit of the protective tariff being then the preservation of a large home market for the home labour, and the prevention of the entry of goods at slaughter prices for a time in order to destroy the domestic manufacturers.[1]

The great aim of statesmen under modern systems of fiscal policy is to increase exports.

[1] The inference that the cost to the consumers of the taxed product is increased not only by the amount of the duty, but also by the distributor's profit on that duty, is not borne out by facts. The glass of beer or spirits does not change in price with changes in the excise duty, nor has the price of bread changed with variations in the price of wheat which exceed that of an import duty. There is a possible change of price as set forth in this chapter and also a re-adjustment of profits among the several distributors when a duty is imposed or withdrawn, but there is no basis for the generalisation that these increase or decrease their charges by twenty-five per cent. upon the amount of the duty in addition to the duty.

Every effort is put forth with this object in view, and the increase of the exports of a country is to some extent the test of its increased prosperity. In forming a plan of a Customs Union for the British Empire, it is very probable that the material advantages which it would confer will be gauged from its tendency to increase the exports of the respective portions of the Empire. The aim of the people of Great Britain would be to obtain such a change of the Colonial tariffs as would promote increased exports from the United Kingdom to the Colonies, and the aim of the Colonies would be to adopt such a policy as would increase their exports.

Exports from the Colonies.

Let us consider first the exports from the Colonies to the United Kingdom. The principal products of the Australasian Colonies are wheat, mutton, skins, tallow, leather, metals, and wool. Those of Canada are wheat, flour, and other grain products, live stock, fish, cheese, eggs, fruits, coal, wood, and furs. The following table gives the quantities of each of the more important of these products imported into the United Kingdom for the yearly average during 1890-91-92, from all the British possessions and from foreign countries respectively, and gives also the percentage which the chief imports from the British possessions bear to the total imports for the years 1890, 1891, and 1892:—

Imports into the United Kingdom, 1890-91-92.[1]

Import.	From British Possessions.	From Foreign Countries.	Percentage of Imports from British Possessions to Total Average.
	Australian Specialties.		
Wheat	£6,726,662	£19,236,655	26%
Mutton	1,985,359	1,406,984	58½%
Leather (undressed)	2,637,579	1,075,600	71%
Hides (dry)	789,991	317,801	71%
Skins	1,471,604	793,265	65%
Tallow	839,826	908,670	48%
Wool	23,996,067	3,212,809	88%
	Canadian Specialties.		
Fish	£564,503	£1,350,458	30%
Wood	4,147,678	13,135,184	24%
Animals	1,780,268	7,656,769	19%
Cheese	2,201,316	2,867,124	43%
Furs	813,517	719,193	53%
Wheat	See above	See above	26%
Wheat flour	664,428	9,831,114	6½%

It will be seen that eighty-eight per cent. of the total imports of wool in those years came from the British possessions, so that an import duty upon foreign wool into the United Kingdom, even if made prohibitive, could only increase the quantity from the British possessions by about twelve per cent. In some years the imports of wool from the

[1] From the *Imperial Institute Year Book*, 1894.

British possessions have amounted to ninety per cent., which leaves only ten per cent. from foreign countries. It is not likely therefore that an import duty on wool would in any perceptible degree increase the trade of the Colonies. We are therefore restricted to the other articles above mentioned in which to promote an increased trade by means of the import duty. Of these articles wheat and flour, cheese and mutton, tallow, hides and skins include specialties of each of the self-governing Colonies, and a differential import duty upon these articles coming into the United Kingdom from foreign countries, say to the extent of fifteen per cent., would be considered a beneficial tariff by all of them.

The Dominion of Canada, Victoria, South Australia and New Zealand export large quantities of wheat and flour. In addition, Canada exports cheese, New Zealand and New South Wales export mutton, all the Australian colonies, New Zealand and the South African colonies export hides, skins and tallow; Tasmania alone does no export trade in any of these seven articles. If the Australasian Colonies were federated the united commonwealth would be a large exporter of all of these products except cheese.

The import duty to be an adequate stimulus to the export trade of the Colonies should be not less than fifteen per cent., the duty of two per cent. or

IMPERIAL TARIFFS. 51

five per cent. proposed by some writers being too small to induce the Colonies to change their fiscal system. It might be necessary, however, to fix the import duty on tallow, hides and skins at five per cent., because they are the raw materials of manufacture.

A Customs Union of the British Empire should, therefore, be formed upon the basis of free trade in these seven articles throughout the British Empire, with a differential tariff of fifteen or even ten per cent. against foreign countries, and it might gradually be extended to include the other articles of Colonial export as well, *viz.*, timber, leather, furs, butter, fish, live stock and grain of all kinds.

The following tables give the average imports for 1890-1-2 into the United Kingdom of the specified articles from foreign countries and British possessions respectively and show the amount of the proposed duty on each. The duty on imports from the British possessions is the measure of the advantage conferred upon the Colonies by this fiscal union.

Imports of Foreign Food and other Products into the United Kingdom for 1890-1-2, *yearly averages.*

Wheat	£19,236,655
Wheat flour	9,831,114
	£29,067,769
Duty 15 per cent.	£4,360,165
„ 10 „	2,906,777

52 IMPERIAL CUSTOMS UNION.

Add cheese	2,867,124	
	£31,934,893	
Duty 15 per cent.		£4,790,233
„ 10 „		3,193,489
Add mutton	1,406,934	
	£33,341,827	
Duty 15 per cent.		5,001,274
„ 10 „		3,341,827
Add hides	317,801	
„ skins	793,265	
	£34,452,893	
Duty 15 per cent.		5,167,934
„ 10 „		3,445,288
Add tallow	908,670	
	£35,361,563	
Duty 15 per cent.		5,304,235
„ 10 „		3,536,156
Add fish	1,350,458	
	£36,712,021	
Duty 15 per cent.		5,506,803
„ 10 „		3,671,201
Add leather	1,075,600	
	£37,787,621	
Duty 15 per cent.		5,668,143
„ 10 „		3,778,761
Add live stock	7,656,769	
	£45,444,390	
Duty 15 per cent.		6,816,658
„ 10 „		4,544,439
Add wood and timber	13,135,184	
	£58,579,574	
Duty 15 per cent.		8,786,936
„ 10 „		5,857,957

IMPERIAL TARIFFS. 53

Imports from British Possessions of Colonial Specialties into the United Kingdom for the average of 1890-1-2.

Wheat	£6,726,662	
Wheat flour	677,762	
	£7,404,424	
Duty 15 per cent.		£1,110,663
„ 10 „		740,442
Add cheese	2,201,316	
„ mutton	1,985,359	
	£11,591,099	
Duty 15 per cent.		1,738,664
„ 10 „		1,159,109
Add hides	789,991	
„ skins	1,471,604	
	£13,852,694	
Duty 15 per cent.		2,077,904
„ 10 „		1,385,269
Add tallow	839,826	
	£14,692,520	
Duty 15 per cent.		2,203,878
„ 10 „		1,469,252
Add fish	564,503	
	£15,257,023	
Duty 15 per cent.		2,288,553
„ 10 „		1,525,702
Add leather	2,637,579	
	£17,894,602	
Duty 15 per cent.		2,684,190
„ 10 „		1,789,460

Add animals (live stock) . 1,780,268

	£19,674,870	
Duty 15 per cent.		£2,951,230
„ 10 „		1,967,487
Add wood and timber .	4,147,124	
	£23,822,548	
Duty 15 per cent.		3,573,382
„ 10 „		2,382,254

The total imports of these seven articles, wheat, flour, cheese, mutton, tallow, hides and skins, for the yearly average of 1890-1-2 from foreign countries, as shown in the above table, amounted to about £35,400,000, upon which a fifteen per cent. duty is £5,304,233 and a ten per cent. duty is £3,536,156. If this duty were collected, a proportionate reduction of taxation could be made in other articles. The principles of free trade would in no way be infringed if at the same time the Colonies made a yearly grant to the United Kingdom equal to fifteen per cent. upon the imports of these seven articles from the Colonies, and if an excise duty equal to fifteen per cent. were imposed also upon the home product. The imports of these seven articles from the British possessions into the United Kingdom for the yearly average of 1890-1-2 amounted to nearly £15,000,000, upon which a fifteen per cent. duty is £2,200,000 and a ten per cent. duty £1,469,252. It has been proposed in a preceding part of this paper that the Colonies should contribute £1,000,000 annually to Imperial defence partly in exchange for this differential tariff. This leaves a balance of £1,200,000 per annum paid by the United Kingdom as a protective bonus if the price of these articles is increased by the total amount of the tax, and if the imports from the Colonies remain the same as in 1891.[1] But a protective tariff of fifteen per cent. would so stimulate the production of these articles in the Colonies that they could supply the total demand of the Mother Country, and the price eventually would not be at all increased. The illimitable prairie fields of Canada, the vast sheep and cattle stations of Australasia, the table-lands of South Africa and the wheat-fields of India are

[1] If the Customs Union were extended to include the remaining Colonial specialties, leather, fish, animals, wood and timber, the duty upon these foreign imports into the United Kingdom would be increased to £8,786,000 and the benefits to the Colonies by the free entry of all these taxed products would amount to £3,500,000 annually. The protective bonus in that case would be increased from £1,200,000 to £2,500,000 yearly. If the duty were reduced to ten per cent. the amount collected upon these foreign imports would be £5,857,957, and the benefit to the Colonies £2,382,254 upon all these specialties, about the same as the fifteen per cent. on the seven articles. This enlarged Customs Union would be more beneficial to the Empire but more difficult of adoption.

capable of supplying the entire wants of the Mother Country. Their mutual competition will be sufficiently keen to reduce the price practically to the same level as though they had to meet foreign competition as well. This is applying upon a large scale, and in the case of these seven articles those principles of assistance to nascent industries which John Stuart Mill and his followers admit as consistent with the principles of free trade. For here we have an industry, that of wheat and cattle raising, which can be carried on upon British territory as cheaply and profitably as in foreign countries. The obstacles to the adequate increase of this industry are the lack of population in some of the Colonies, and of irrigation and railway facilities in others. Time and the temporary restriction of foreign competition would attract the population where it is deficient and would supply the required facilities where they are lacking; ultimately the full supply would be furnished from within the Empire without any increase of cost. This result and the advantage of being independent of foreign countries for food supplies in time of war justify a temporary duty even on free-trade principles.

The protection afforded to the agriculture of Great Britain by such a tariff may be justified upon several grounds. First, as a war tax to make this country in time of war less dependent upon foreign countries for its food supply; secondly, to offset the local taxation upon land, which under the present system amounts to a bounty in favour of foreign growers of these products, *i.e.*, the English farmer is handicapped in his competition with the foreign and Colonial producer to the extent to which his land contributes to the taxation of this country, in addition to the taxes he pays in common with other citizens. Thirdly, the preservation of the special skill and capital which have been applied to agriculture in Great Britain would also be a gain of some value from an import duty on bread-stuffs. This industry is declining so rapidly that it threatens soon to become non-existent. It may be questioned whether the advantages which manufacturing industries may derive from the continuance of free trade in bread-stuffs will not be dearly purchased by the extinction of home agriculture. The agitation which is now being excited in favour of a bounty to British wheat growers is an indication that the adoption of a project such as is here outlined would not be so difficult as the extreme free traders assume.

It will, of course, be objected that the prosperity of Great Britain is due to her manufacturing supremacy, which is dependent upon her food supplies being obtained at the cheapest possible price, and that a tax of fifteen or even of ten per cent. upon food and products would to this extent diminish her power of competing with foreign countries in neutral markets. But the extent to which a duty of fifteen per cent. upon these four articles of food supply, wheat, flour, mutton and cheese, would increase the expense of manufacturing has been greatly exaggerated. Firstly, if the cost of the manufactures of Great Britain and Ireland, estimated at £400,000,000, or even if the cost of the total exports, say £300,000,000, were increased (which it is not) by an amount equal to fifteen per cent. upon the value of the total quantity of these four products consumed in the United Kingdom, and not imported from foreign countries, it would be so slight a percentage, probably not more than one to one and a half per cent. upon the total manufactured product of the United Kingdom, as not appreciably to affect the power of Great Britain to hold its own in foreign markets.[1] But only a

---

[1] The fifteen per cent. duty on wheat, and mutton, flour, cheese, tallow, hides and skins, imported from British possessions is shown in table, p. 53, as - - - - £2,202,028
Do. on value of home-grown wheat, p. 61, - 806,911
Do. on value of home-made cheese, and mutton, tallow, hides and skins (estimated at forty-five per cent. the total consumption, as shown by Mr. Stephen Bourne), - - 1,700,000
                                                        £4,708,939

proportion, and that not the largest proportion, of this total quantity is consumed in manufacturing. All that portion which is consumed by persons living upon their incomes from investments, or upon incomes from fixed fees, and by persons whose work does not directly or indirectly concern manufacturers, has no effect in increasing the cost of manufactured products. The duty upon tallow, hides and skins might at first injure the trades requiring these products, but would not otherwise affect general manufacturing.

Secondly, as has been shown above, the increased price, if any, of the foreign importations which actually pay the duty, is offset by a decrease in the price of other things upon which the taxes may be reduced. For instance, the duty upon beer is practically as much of a tax upon manufacturing as would be a duty upon any of the products herein mentioned, and it would be possible to reduce the duty upon beer, and consequently the price of beer, to the extent to which the Treasury is benefited by the duty upon the seven articles above mentioned. It is, of course, argued that a duty upon beer conduces to the morality of

This is only one and a half per cent. upon the value of the annual exports from the United Kingdom and about three-quarters per cent. upon the trade profits upon which income tax is paid. A ten per cent. duty would be still less.

the people, but beer is simply mentioned as an illustration, and the reduction of taxation may be made on any other taxed product, such as tea, currants, coffee and raisins, which yielded about £4,000,000 of revenue in 1894-5.

Thirdly, the certainty that the British possessions can ultimately supply the total wants of the British Empire in these seven products as cheaply as other countries, and the stimulus given to Colonial production by this duty, ensure that the price of these products *will not be increased* to the extent of the duty imposed upon the foreign product.

Fourthly, the resultant extent to which the cost of manufacturing will be increased by this duty may be regarded in the light partly of an insurance premium against famine in time of war, and partly as the cost of the increased unity and the consequent increased stability of the British Empire.

The amount of the increased cost of home-grown wheat, caused by an import duty, is clearly indicated by the following estimate. The yield of the wheat crop of Great Britain for 1895 is estimated by the Board of Agriculture at 4,647,000 quarters. Of this, 500,000 quarters are required for seed, leaving 4,147,000 quarters for consumption. Adding 200,000 quarters for Ireland makes the total wheat crop of the United Kingdom for 1895

IMPERIAL TARIFFS. 61

for consumption—4,347,000 quarters. The average price of wheat for the twelve months ending 30th April, 1896, was 24/9 per quarter, which gives the total value of the wheat crop, £5,379,412, upon which the duty would amount to £806,911. If a duty of fifteen per cent. gave such a stimulus to agriculture that the wheat crop of the United Kingdom would be doubled, the value would only amount to £10,000,000. A duty of fifteen per cent. upon this value gives £1,500,000, which is the maximum increased cost of home-grown wheat due to this protective tariff. If the price were increased by the full amount of the duty, which is not likely, and if the production were increased twofold, which would be surprising (the average production of 1891-2-3 was 7,000,000 quarters [1]), this increased price considered as a war premium against famine is insignificant and amounts only to an increase of five per cent. in our total expenditure for defence. As increasing the total cost of our manufactures it is infinitesimal.

[1] The official return of the wheat crop of the United Kingdom for the years specified is as follows:—

		Average price.
1892, 60,775,000 bushels,	-	30/3.
1893, 50,913,000 „	-	26/4.
1894, 60,705,000 „	-	22/10.
1895, 38,708,000 „	-	24/9.
yearly average, 52,775,250 „	-	26/.

about 6,597,000 quarters.

Imports of Specialties into the Colonies.

As an Imperial Customs Union in these seven products requires the imports of them into the Colonies to have the same duty as into the United Kingdom, it is necessary to consider shortly its effect upon their importation into the Colonies. The following table gives the quantities imported of the principal of these products into the leading Colonies, and shows that a change from the present duties upon these imports from all sources, to a duty of fifteen or even ten per cent. upon importations from abroad, and free entry for importations from the British possessions, would be insignificant compared with the advantage to be derived from a Customs Union and from the preferential command of the home market.

Bread-stuffs imported and exported in Australasian Colonies. Wheat, flour and biscuits (flour reduced to bushels). Annual average of 1891-2-3.[1]

Colony.	Imported Bushels.	Exported Bushels.	Excess of Bushels.
Victoria	313,294	6,448,520	Exp. 6,135,226
New South Wales	2,886,028	388,442	Imp. 2,497,586
Queensland	1,828,786	4,747	Imp. 1,824,039
South Australia	294,668	6,550,728	Exp. 6,256,060
Western Australia.	221,668	None	Imp. 221,668
Tasmania	153,524	1,614	Imp. 151,910
New Zealand	2,235	2,337,324	Exp. 2,335,089
	5,700,203	15,731,375	
Total Excess of Exports			. 10,030,937

[1] From Colonial Blue Books.

IMPERIAL TARIFFS.

Imports of 1891.[1]

Colony.	Wheat. Value Imported.	Wheat. Amount of Duties Collected.	Flour. Value Imported.	Flour. Amount of Duties Collected.	Cheese. Value Imported.	Cheese. Amount of Duties Collected.	Proportion of Foreign Cheese.
Victoria	£55,719	£7	£15,649	£6	£4,162	£1,212	14%
New South Wales	194,909	645	703,297	1,379	9,231	792	33%
Queensland	55,659	Free	353,593	Free	19,774	12,104	1%
S. Australia	7,253	114		None	4,836	358	4%
W. Australia	17,376	2,316	48,323	4,826	7,064	2,965	
New Zealand	400				80		
Tasmania	41,482	5,090	5,227	677	237	44	
Cape Colony	210,528	52,221	21,787	6,232	35,551	13,705	8%
Natal	51	2	167,167	7,720	13,557	3,640	25%
Canada (for home consumption)	30,026	5,670	122,608	17,950	4,520	766	14%
Total	613,403	66,065	1,437,651	38,790	99,012	35,586	

Canadian imports are estimated at $5 to the £1 sterling. No complete statistics of mutton, tallow, hides and skins are available, but the imports of these into the Colonies are not important. Imports of flour and wheat into Australasian and South African Colonies are almost all from British possessions. Imports of flour and wheat into Canada are almost all from foreign countries.

[1] From Colonial Blue Books.

As the imports of these products into Canada are entirely from foreign countries, upon which the duties in 1891 were almost exactly fifteen per cent., the change would practically not be noticeable. The imports into Victoria, New South Wales, Queensland, South Australia and New Zealand are wholly from British possessions, and as the duties collected at present upon them are very small, the loss of revenue from their free entry under a Customs Union is too slight to be taken into account.

The exceptions are Western Australia, Tasmania and South Africa. As these South African Colonies derive a large revenue from their import duty on wheat, cheese and flour, all of which come from the British possessions, they would require to obtain a revenue from some other source to make up for its loss under a Customs Union. But as they are free-trade Colonies, with no opposing protection influence, and as only about five per cent. of their customs revenue is derived from these articles, this could easily be arranged by the increase of differential duties on other imports. If the Australian Colonies were first combined in a federation of their own, they would practically supply themselves with all these products and no revenue would be raised upon their import. This loss of revenue amounting to £10,000 in Western Australia, and £5811 in Tasmania, which is less than four per cent. of the total customs revenue, would require to be made up from other sources, and this could be accomplished by the differential duties proposed in the next chapter and by the increased prosperity due to the Australian federation and to the Imperial Customs Union.

CHAPTER VI.

COLONIAL TARIFFS.

THE fiscal policy above set forth combines ideal simplicity with thorough effectiveness. It establishes a Customs Union with absolute free trade throughout the Empire in seven most important Colonial products, and it stimulates Colonial trade by imposing a differential duty of fifteen per cent. upon the import of these seven articles from all foreign countries into any part of the British Empire. This union is accomplished with a minimum of change, a facility of operation, and an avoidance of confusion which are the essential characteristics of a successful scheme of tariff reform. The duties imposed are few in number, and are easily collected. They produce about £5,000,000 annually; which makes it possible to place five other taxed articles on the free list with a corresponding reduction of taxation. The disturbance caused in either the Imperial or the Colonial revenue system is inappreciable, while the results are most important and far-reaching. But the benefit is almost wholly with the Colonies. The other part of this plan of union, however, gives an equivalent preponderating advantage to the United Kingdom, as will now be set forth in detail.

In like manner as the exports from the Colonies will be stimulated by the preferential tariff herein advocated, so the exports from the United Kingdom will be promoted by a differential tariff in the British possessions in favour of imports into them from the United Kingdom. This preferential tariff must be a benefit both absolutely and relatively, *i.e.*, it should reduce the duties on British manufactures imported into the Colonies from that now in force; and it should also reduce these duties as compared with imports from foreign countries. The former will enable the British manufacturer to compete upon more equal terms than he does at present with the local manufacturer in the Colonies, as well as with the importer from foreign countries. The amount of this reduction must be a matter of mutual arrangement.

The following table gives the percentage of the total imports of each group of Colonies for the years 1885 and 1891 which each group received from the United Kingdom, the British possessions, and foreign countries respectively.

	From		
Into	United Kingdom.	British Possessions.	Foreign Countries.
In 1885.[1]			
Australasia	51·00	38·30	10·70
Canada	39·60	4·40	56·00
South Africa	75·60	11·10	13·30
India	70·50	11·40	18·11
In 1891.[2]			
Canada	35·08	\multicolumn{2}{c}{64·92}	
Australasia	43·00	46·70	10·40
South Africa	83·00	\multicolumn{2}{c}{19·00}	

This table shows that in Australasia and South Africa the imports from foreign countries in 1885 were about one-fifth of those from the United Kingdom, while in Canada they were one-half more. Since that date the foreign trade of the Colonies has been increasing more rapidly than that with the Mother Country, and those proportions are now even more favourable to foreign countries. The total foreign trade of the British possessions with foreign countries has increased

[1] From Rawson's Tables.   [2] From Blue Books.

in a greater ratio than that with the United Kingdom, which has been steadily decreasing, as the following table exhibits.

Proportion of the trade with the United Kingdom to the total foreign trade of the British possessions.

	Per cent.
1871	51·41
1875	52·33
1880	49·36
1884	46·72
1885	48·44
1886	45·31
1887	44·14
1888	47·76
1889	47·71
1890	46·51
1891	45·65
1892	47·33
1893	44·68 [1]

The next table gives the amount of the exports of the United Kingdom for 1891 for each of the chief divisions of articles (made by the Board of Trade), with the percentage of such exports sent to the British possessions.

[1] From the *Statistical Year Book of Canada*, 1894, p. 621.

Exports from the United Kingdom for 1891 *of the produce and manufactures of the United Kingdom, with the proportion sent to the British possessions.*[1]

Articles.	Value.	Percentage sent to British Possessions.
Cotton Manufactures	£60,230,256	44
,, Yarn	11,177,348	26
Woollen Manufactures	18,446,640	28
Woollen and Worsted Yarn	3,910,651	2½
Linen Manufactures	5,032,196	17
Jute ,,	2,561,872	10
Apparel and Haberdashery	7,151,032	80
Iron and Steel Manufactures	26,877,000	37
Hardware and Cutlery	2,527,575	50
Copper	3,828,112	2½
Machinery	15,817,515	25
Coal, Cinders, Fuel, etc.	18,895,078	12
Chemicals	8,877,712	20
Average proportion sent to British Possessions		30
Proportion sent to self-governing Colonies		15

These tables show that thirty per cent. of the total exports of the United Kingdom go to the British possessions, of which about fifteen per cent. go to the self-governing Colonies, and that foreign countries are gradually getting a larger share of the Colonial trade at the expense of the British trader. The chief articles the export of which may be stimu-

[1] From *Imperial Institute Year Book, Statesman's Year Book,* and *Official Blue Book.*

lated by a Colonial preferential tariff are cotton manufactures, woollen manufactures, hardware and cutlery, and iron and steel manufactures, including machinery. An Imperial Customs Union must therefore include a second group of articles of commerce upon which uniform, or nearly uniform, duties shall be levied in the self-governing Colonies, comprising the principal of the above-mentioned articles. As a considerable proportion of the revenue of the Colonies is at present derived from the import duties on these articles it would not be possible to induce them to abolish such duties entirely, but they might establish a maximum and a minimum tariff; the maximum tariff to apply to imports from foreign countries, the minimum tariff to be levied wholly upon articles coming from the United Kingdom. The maximum tariff should be about ten per cent. in excess of the minimum tariff, and be carefully arranged upon the various articles so as to cause the least inconvenience. It should be so imposed that the average difference shall amount to ten per cent., and shall constitute as nearly as possible a reduction of five per cent. on the average in favour of imports from Great Britain as compared with the present tariffs.

Rates of Duties levied on Imports into several Colonies, 1891 to 1892.[1]

	Cotton Manufactures.	Woollen Manufactures.	Hardware, Cutlery, Iron and Steel.	Machinery.	Linen.
Australasia:—					
New South Wales	Free	Free, some 10%	Free to 10% and specific duty	Free to 10%	Free to 10%
Victoria	Free	Free to 40%	Free to 35%	Free to 35%	Free to 35%
S. Australia	Free	10 to 15%	Free to 25%	Free to 25%	Free
W. Australia	10%	5 to 10%	Free to 15% and specific duty	5%	5 to 10%
Tasmania	12½%.	15%	Free to 15% and specific duty	5 to 7½%	12½ to 20%
N. Zealand	Some free, others 10%	20%	Free to 25% and specific duty	Free to 20%	25%
Queensland	5%	5 to 15%	Free to 25% and specific duty	Free to 25%	25%
Natal	5 to 15%	5 to 15%	Free to 5%	Free to 5%	5 to 15%
Cape of Good Hope	12%	12%	Free to 12%	Free to 2%	12%
Canada	15 to 25% and 1% per yard	20 to 27½% plus specific duties	12½ to 35% and specific duty	10 to 35%	5 to 20%

[1] From the *Statistical Abstract for* 1893.

It will be seen from the above table that a differential duty of ten per cent. is sufficient for Cape Colony, Natal, Queensland, New South Wales, Western Australia, Tasmania and New Zealand, in which the import duties rarely exceed fifteen per cent., and there is not much margin for reduction. In Canada, Victoria and South Australia the import duties are higher, and the change to a differential tariff should be a reduction of ten per cent. in favour of the United Kingdom as compared with the present tariff. As the tendency of popular feeling in these Colonies is in favour of a moderate reduction of tariff, this change is quite practicable as part of a Customs Union.

The Colonial tariffs are so dissimilar and have been framed upon such different plans that no general principle applicable to all of them can be established. The proposed reductions must be arranged according to the special circumstances of each Colony, and these can only be determined by their respective Legislatures, subject to the approval of the Imperial Government. The important point to be insisted on is that British imports, if dutiable, shall be subject to ten per cent. lower duty than imports from foreign countries, and this presents no serious obstacle. The advantage accruing to the United Kingdom from this ten per cent. reduction is indicated by the following table, and amounts to £826,000 annually, upon the basis of the duties of 1894.

Import Duties collected in Colonies, 1894.[1]

In	Total Import Duties.	Duties Collected on British Imports.	Ten per cent. reduction.
Canada	£3,875,964	£1,650,000	£165,000
Australasia	£7,655,749	estimated £5,360,000	£536,000
Cape Colony, Natal	£1,668,303	£1,250,000	£125,000
Total	£13,200,016	£8,260,000	£826,000

In fixing these respective differences of tariff it would not be necessary for each group of Colonies to have precisely identical tariffs upon these articles, but they might be arranged to suit the circumstances of each group, provided the differences were not so great that it would induce shipments from foreign countries to the Colony with the cheapest duties and thence to the Colony having the higher duties. It will be objected—

1. That it is difficult for these Colonies to reduce their import duties from the United Kingdom

[1] The duties on British imports into Australasia are estimated by taking the percentage of these duties to the total Customs duties collected in New Zealand, which are given accurately for that Colony, and applying the same percentage to the Customs duties of the other Australasian Colonies which do not give separately the duties upon British imports.

because of revenue requirements. But it may be pointed out—

(*a*) That the foreign trade of the Australasian Colonies is growing much more rapidly than their trade with the British Empire, and that in arranging the difference of the maximum and minimum tariff an average reduction of, say, three per cent. might be sufficient, combined with an increase of seven per cent. upon imports from foreign countries, in all the Australasian Colonies except Victoria and South Australia.

(*b*) That South Africa has not a protective tariff, and that the preferential tariff in favour of Great Britain might be arranged with reference solely to revenue purposes by a greater increase of duty upon foreign imports, the same as suggested for Australasia. These are details which a spirit of conciliation and a desire to obtain the advantages of the Customs Union would arrange.

(*c*) That there is a strong sentiment in Canada for a reduction of duties, and for a preferential tariff applicable to the British Empire, and the time is opportune for applying such a reduction as the country now demands to imports from Great Britain in connection with the import duty on bread-stuffs into the United Kingdom as proposed herein.

(*d*) That a reduction of duty is usually accompanied by an increase of importation, and up to a certain point there would be no loss of revenue.

2. It may be objected that the Colonial Governments would decline to alter their tariffs for the benefit of Great Britain, but under the present system of legislation in the British Empire the Parliaments of the self-governing Colonies are obliged to consult the wishes of the Imperial Parliament with respect to quite a number of subjects, as coinage, copyright, merchant shipping, and the avoidance of differential tariffs against the Mother Country in favour of foreign countries. It would not be more difficult for these same Legislatures to avoid legislating upon those special features of Imperial policy which an Imperial conference should in the course of a few years decide to be essential to the unity of the Empire.

3. It is further objected that a differential tariff throughout the British Empire against foreign countries would induce retaliation by them, and that it would be necessary for Great Britain to denounce her present treaties of commerce with Belgium and Germany. It cannot be alleged under our present system that any foreign country shows Great Britain or her Colonies any favour. They have at present, almost without exception, as hostile tariffs as it is possible for them to have, consistent with what

they consider the interest of their own commerce. It is possible that at first a feeling of irritation might cause foreign countries to enact a higher retaliatory tariff if the treaties of commerce permitted it; but as they at present refrain from doing so, not out of consideration for Great Britain, but from a sense of the injury it would cause to their own business interests, it would only require a very short time for the citizens of the foreign country prejudicially affected to make their influence felt in the withdrawal of the objectionable measures. Besides, other countries include their Colonies in free-trade relations with themselves and in protective tariffs against the outside world. Algiers and Tunis in that way favour France as against foreign countries. Alsace-Lorraine and Heligoland are now comprised in the Customs Union with the other parts of the German Empire and under a protective tariff against foreign countries. Alaska is also included in the protective tariff of the United States. There would, therefore, be no real ground of complaint against Great Britain for entering into a Customs Union with her Colonies, and the feeling of irritation would soon pass away when the reasonableness of this policy came to be fully understood.

The despatch of Lord Ripon upon his vacation of office last summer respecting Colonial trade sets forth very strongly the disadvantages which the denunciation of the treaties with Belgium and Germany for the benefit of the Colonies would entail upon Great Britain. He shows that the trade of Great Britain with Belgium and Germany is so large in proportion to that with the self-governing Colonies that it would be suicidal for her to denounce these treaties, and he expresses the belief that neither of these countries is willing for the British Colonies to be withdrawn from its operation. These treaties provide that the produce of these countries, Belgium and Germany, shall receive in the British Colonies no worse fiscal treatment than the produce of the United Kingdom. The Belgian treaty declares that "articles the produce or manufactures of Belgium shall not be subject, in the British Colonies, to other or higher duties than those which are or may be imposed upon similar articles of British origin". The treaty with Germany has a clause to the same effect. The objections which the Colonies have to these treaties are that it obliges them to treat Great Britain in the same way as foreign countries, and to give to Belgium and Germany precisely the same treatment as they give to the United Kingdom. The "favoured nation" clause in treaties of commerce with other countries obliges Great Britain to extend the advantages which she has accorded to Belgium

COLONIAL TARIFFS. 79

and Germany under their treaties of commerce to those other countries; therefore the treaties with Belgium and Germany prevent Great Britain from giving her Colonies any fiscal advantage which all other countries having commercial treaties with Great Britain cannot also claim.

The Earl of Ripon states that without this clause including the Colonies in the operation of the treaties, those two nations are not willing to continue them. The position therefore is, that in order to obtain or to continue an advantageous treaty with Belgium and Germany, Great Britain has included the Colonies, or continues to include the Colonies against their wishes, and contrary to their supposed interests. It is doubtless a fact that Belgium and Germany prefer to include the Colonies in their treaties with Great Britain, and they are quite within their rights in objecting most strongly to the withdrawal of the British Colonies from their operation. But it is not so manifest that they would acquiesce in the abrogation of this treaty if it were restricted to Great Britain alone, and it is a matter of certainty that they would renew it, in any case, though perhaps on less advantageous terms to Great Britain in other respects. The inestimable advantages of Imperial unity warrant the incurring of that risk, and it may be doubted whether the equity of the case justifies Great Britain in sacrificing the interests of the Empire for her own advantage in continuing the Colonies under these treaties against their wishes. In fact this statement may be put more strongly. The principles of British Colonial government do not justify the continuance of these treaties which compel the British Colonies against their interests to give foreign countries exceptional treatment such as no other nation exacts from its Colonies, and the plea that the clause imposing this obligation upon the British Colonies is necessary in order to obtain the favourable terms for Great Britain afforded by these treaties is not a sufficient reason for thus reversing the established principles of Colonial government which we have so long practised, nor is it worthy of the paramount power in the Empire.

One of the advantages of this Customs Union is that though it begins with free trade in only a few articles, there can be no question but that it will eventually lead to complete free trade throughout the Empire. This of itself would be an inestimable advantage from the point of view of the advocates of free trade. And we have seen in our sketch of the Customs Unions of the past that their development has always been in the direction of increasing the free trade area comprised within the union. As the Colonies become more intimately associated in trade affairs with the Mother Country, her influence will be exerted more and more powerfully in favour of Imperial free trade. The protective Colonies will gradually come to appreciate its advantages as practised throughout the Empire reciprocally, and adopt it more and more completely. This partial Customs Union will be the germ of a perfect Customs Union with complete free trade within the Empire, and a uniform tariff against the outside world. It might also compel foreign countries to grant reciprocal free trade.

The more intimate relations established by the management of this Customs Union will beget a closer feeling of union than could be created in any other way. Each part will be considered as essential to the whole, as the foot or the hand is to the human body. Each part will consequently make as great sacrifices for any other portion of the Empire as for itself. The added strength which this union of feeling will give to the whole is immeasurable. Increased trade and prosperity may be expected from this more intimate union. The proverb, "Trade follows the flag," has been stated more accurately by Lord Playfair as "Financial confidence follows the flag". The union of the various portions of the British Empire by a stronger and more lasting bond must also beget greater financial confidence, and we may add to the proverb and say, "Financial confidence follows union and the flag".

CHAPTER VII.

THE CONSTITUTION OF THE IMPERIAL CUSTOMS UNION.

THE practicability of a British Imperial Customs Union having been established in the preceding pages, it is necessary in conclusion to state briefly the measures which must be taken in order to place it upon a thorough working basis. They may be set forth in the following order :—

1. The Imperial Government shall summon a conference of Imperial and Colonial delegates to meet in London for the purpose of elaborating the details of an agreement between the Mother Country and the various Colonies. This agreement should be for a fixed period—not less than ten years—and should comprise—

(a) An undertaking by the Imperial Government to expend a definite sum in increasing the effectiveness of the navy, and in strengthening the strategic points which command the lines of communication between the Mother Country and the Colonies. The present Government have applied a portion of their surplus this year for this purpose, and it is admitted almost universally that the safety of the Empire requires an addition to the strength of our navy and its bases, whether the Colonies join in bearing their share, or not. It is suggested that this amount should not be less than £10,000,000, spread over several years.

(*b*) The various Colonies should agree to pay an annual subvention towards the cost of maintaining the strategic points above mentioned, and this subvention should be not less than £1,000,000 per annum throughout the whole term of the agreement.

The proportions to be paid by the respective Colonies to be determined either *pro rata* to population or to revenue, or to imports and exports, as may be deemed most equitable. It might be advisable to form a scale of contribution which shall be determined by all three of the above-mentioned factors instead of by any one of them.

(*c*) The Mother Country should bind herself to impose during the continuance of this agreement an import duty of ten or fifteen per cent. upon such food and other products as may be decided upon which are imported into the United Kingdom being the produce of foreign countries, and to admit free of any duty all such products as shall be imported being the produce of the British possessions. The products suggested should be: Wheat, flour, cheese and mutton, tallow, hides and skins, with the possible addition of live animals, fresh or frozen meats, fish, leather, furs and timber. Other articles might be included which would benefit those Colonies whose exports do not include the above products.

(*d*) The Colonies should undertake in consideration of the advantages above conferred to make a differential tariff in favour of imports into the Colonies being the produce and manufactures of the United Kingdom, of, say, ten per cent. as compared with the tariff imposed upon imports from foreign countries. And this differential tariff should apply to manufactures of cotton, wool, linen, iron and steel, with a provision for its being extended to all other imports, should it be found practicable when the experience of the working of this preferential tariff in these articles has accustomed the Colonies to this system.

The delegates to this conference should be invited from all the self-governing Colonies, and also from India and the leading Crown Colonies, but it is essential that the agreement should apply at least to the principal self-governing Colonies. The initiative in this conference should be taken by the Imperial Government, which should undertake to recommend the proposed British concessions to the Imperial Parliament.

This first conference should decide as to establishing itself as a permanent institution having annual or biennial meetings, and as to its

CONSTITUTION OF THE UNION. 85

powers. These should include the consideration of the extension of the tariff arrangements set forth in sub-sections (c) and (d) and the altering of any tariff inequalities which bear unequally or oppressively upon any individual Colony. It should also consider questions of Imperial defence, and the strengthening against external attack of such portions of the Empire as may be found by Colonial experience to be dangerously weak. Its decisions may at first be subject to ratification by the respective Legislatures before being carried into execution.

The consideration of questions relating to the encouragement of trade and commerce between the various portions of the British Empire such as foreshadowed in Mr. Chamberlain's recent circular to the Governors of the Colonies might also constitute a function of the conference.

The tendency would be, as time rolled on, for a representative body such as that herein outlined to aggregate to itself other powers and functions in the same way that the British House of Commons has gradually engrossed the management of the constitutional affairs of the Empire.

2. After these questions have been discussed and the conference has passed a resolution in favour of the course above outlined, the Colonial Governments shall be invited to put these resolutions

into effect, in the same way that the resolutions of the Ottawa Conference and of the Conference of 1887 were carried out by the respective Legislatures. It may be that some time will elapse before all the self-governing Colonies shall agree to the provisions of this agreement, or even before the conference will recommend them all. But the advantages are so manifest that they will, without doubt, be ultimately adopted, and the time of their adoption will be greatly hastened should any war excitement arise, such as that caused by the belligerent message of President Cleveland to the United States Congress.

3. Concurrently with the first meeting of the conference, or before, or after, as may be most convenient, a strong effort should be made by the most influential persons in this movement to induce the Australasian Colonies to form a distinct federation, and also to combine all the South African Colonies into one commonwealth. After this is accomplished—and the obstacles do not seem to be insurmountable—there would then be but three groups of self-governing Colonies, *viz.*, the Canadian Dominion, the Australian Confederation, and the South African Commonwealth. It might even be deemed advisable to make the formation of these confederated groups a condition precedent to the granting of the concessions above mentioned by the Imperial Government.

4. A bill should be introduced into the Imperial Parliament and enacted into law, empowering, if necessary, the various Colonial Parliaments and Legislatures to carry out the agreements entered into, as above set forth, and conferring upon the Inter-Colonial Conference such powers as may be essential for the purpose of the duties assigned to them.

Another bill should authorise the execution of an agreement on behalf of the United Kingdom, for the imposing of differential tariffs as finally decided upon by the Inter-Colonial Conference, and for carrying out any other provisions which may be required by the establishment of this Imperial Customs Union.

5. An order in council should be passed authorising the Secretary of State for the Colonies to summon the several Colonial representatives to a Council of Colonial Advice, similar to the Committee on Plantations formerly in operation, and to give the members of this council the right to see all papers respecting Colonial affairs received by the Colonial Office, excepting such communications from the Governors as may be marked "Private and Confidential". The Colonial representatives might also be allowed to address protests or representations to the Secretary of State to be submitted by him to the Imperial Parliament for its consideration; and it might also be found expedient to allow

the Colonial representatives seats in the House of Commons for the purpose of addressing the House upon Colonial questions, without having any vote therein. This Colonial Council should also have the right to have one of their number elected either by themselves or by the conference as a Colonial representative upon the Imperial Committee of Defence. It would strengthen the prestige of this Colonial Committee if the Colonial representatives were called to the Privy Council, and there seems to be no objection to this course.

In the deliberations of this Council of Advice it might be necessary at first for the Secretary of State for the Colonies and the Under-Secretaries of State—who might be made members thereof—to have the controlling influence, but the respective influences of the Colonies and the Mother Country in this Colonial Council should be changed from time to time as experience showed any changes necessary for its effective working. All Imperial questions affecting the Colonies should be submitted for the consideration of this Council of Advice, in the same way that questions relating to trade and commerce are brought before the committee of the Board of Trade. This Colonial Council should also be charged with the administrative work connected with the annual meetings of the inter-Colonial conferences. It should formulate the questions to be discussed by them. It should keep the various Colonial Governments informed as to the meetings of the conferences and the subjects proposed for their consideration. It should be the medium of communication between the Governments of the respective Colonies, and should receive suggestions as to points which any Colonial Government wished to submit to the conference. It should press upon the Colonies the putting into operation the resolutions adopted by the conferences in the same way that a Cabinet urges the adoption by the House of Lords of the bills passed by the Lower House.

No Imperial legislation would probably be required to constitute this Council, or to entrust these duties to it, but if such legislation were required, it must be enacted by the Imperial Parliament. The experience of the working of Cabinets teaches us that while divergence of opinion frequently exists respecting particular questions, yet that the will of the two or three masterful minds who are the leaders of the Cabinet always dominates the others. There is no doubt but that such a Council of Colonial Advice would generally agree upon any course to be adopted, and that the Secretary of State for the Colonies would usually have the controlling influence. His judgments, however, would probably be modified by his colleagues on this Council of Advice, and the influence of the Colony specially affected in any particular case would no doubt have its due predominance. Cases of dissent or divergence, so pronounced as to cause dissension, would have to be decided as at present by the predominant authority of the Imperial Cabinet.

6. The commercial treaties with Belgium and Germany should be denounced unless the clauses restricting the right of the Colonies to give preferential treatment to the Mother Country were voluntarily withdrawn by them.

We have thus sketched an outline of a practical Imperial Customs Union. It is not a rigid paper constitution. The details are subject to change as experience and consultation may suggest. It is a development of forces of government which are already in operation in a rudimentary manner within the British Empire. It presupposes a community of men of average common-sense, whose affairs are managed by statesmen of average prudence and wisdom. This scheme no doubt has many defects; critics may point out difficulties in its working, but equal if not greater difficulties may be shown in every existing constitution, even in those considered most successful. The spirit of conciliation, of patriotic desire for good government, and an earnest endeavour to minimise difficulties, have developed the Saxon Witenagemot into the powerful British House of Commons, have transformed the rigid, inelastic constitution of the United States of America into a comprehensive form of government resting upon the same written basis, but capable of expansion over a whole continent, and have unified a multitúde of petty states into the great German Empire. The same qualities may be relied upon to consolidate by means of these international conferences and this representative Council of Colonial Advice the dominions of Her Imperial Majesty into a great and successful Imperial Customs Union.

www.ingramcontent.com/pod-product-compliance
Lightning Source LLC
Chambersburg PA
CBHW031119160426
43192CB00008B/1040